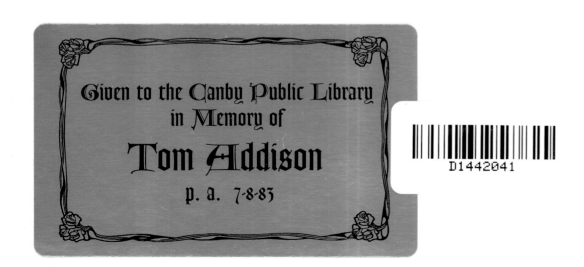

Home Life
IN ANCIENT EGYPT

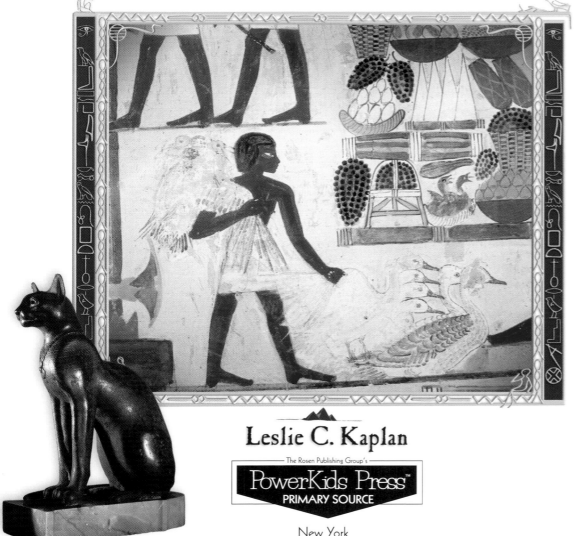

Leslie C. Kaplan

The Rosen Publishing Group's
PowerKids Press™
PRIMARY SOURCE

New York

To Nicole and Steve

Published in 2004 by The Rosen Publishing Group, Inc.

29 East 21st Street, New York, NY 10010

First Edition

Editor: Rachel O'Connor
Book Design: Maria E. Melendez
Photo Researcher: Adriana Skura

Photo Credits: Cover, p. 12 (top) © Werner Forman/Art Resource, NY; cover (inset), pp. 16 (bottom), 20 © Erich Lessing/Art Resource, NY; pp. 4, 20 (right) © Scala/Art Resource, NY; pp. 7, 11 (left) The Art Archive/Musée du Louvre, Paris/Dagli Orti; p. 8 (top) The Art Archive/Luxor Museum, Egypt/Dagli Orti; p. 8 (left) The Art Archive/Musée des Arts Decoratifs, Paris/Dagli Orti; p. 8 (right) The Art Archive/Egyptian Museum, Turin/Dagli Orti; pp.11 (right), 12 (left), 15, 19 The Art Archive/Dagli Orti; pp. 12 (right), 16 (top) The Art Archive/Egyptian Museum, Cairo/Dagli Orti.

Kaplan, Leslie C.
  Home life in ancient Egypt / Leslie C. Kaplan.—1st ed.
    p. cm.—(Primary sources of ancient civilizations. Egypt)
Includes bibliographical references and index.
Contents: Family life—A townhouse—Villas—Marriage—Children—The role of women in the home—Learning young—Meals—Personal hygiene—Religion in the home.
  ISBN 0-8239-6784-0 (library binding)—ISBN 0-8239-8935-6 (pbk.)
1. Egypt—Social life and customs—To 332 B.C.—Juvenile literature. 2. Family—Egypt—Juvenile literature. [1. Egypt—Social life and customs—To 332 B.C. 2. Family—Egypt.] I. Title. II. Series.
  DT61.K3459 2004
  932—dc21
                                                        2002154683

Manufactured in the United States of America

Contents

Family Life   5

A Town House   6

Villas   9

Marriage   10

Children   13

The Role of Women in the Home   14

Learning Young   17

Meals   18

Personal Hygiene   21

Religion in the Home   22

Glossary   23

Index   24

Primary Sources   24

Web Sites   24

This household shrine shows Akhenaton, Nefertiti, and their three daughters worshiping the sun god Aton. The painted limestone image came from the Eighteenth Dynasty (1567–1320 B.C.) and was found near Tell el-Amarna, Egypt.

Family Life

   The ancient Egyptians placed great importance on family life. Although the husband was the head of the household, he treated his wife with love and respect. In many scenes of home life on tombs or in literature, parents are shown to cherish their children. A usual ancient Egyptian family would include four or five children. Pets, such as dogs or monkeys, were common in the Egyptian home. The women would do many of the household chores such as baking bread, cleaning, and sewing. The men worked on the land or as tradesmen, such as carpenters. The family worshiped their gods at home. Only priests and kings were allowed in the temples.

A Town House

Many ancient Egyptian families lived in town houses, which were usually two or three stories high. They were made from mud bricks because wood was scarce and the mud-brick walls were inexpensive to build. The brick lasted for a long time because there was little rainfall in Egypt. The bricks were made from straw mixed with mud from the Nile River and dried in the hot sun. Windows were built high on the walls and were small to help keep the inside of the home cool. A staircase usually led to the rooftop. When the sun made the indoors too hot, the Egyptians would cook and sleep on the roof in the cooler evening air.

Egyptians made furniture using wood and palm leaves. The pieces shown here, which include a chair, a stool, and storage baskets, date from about the Eighteenth Dynasty.

This is a model of a two-story Egyptian house with a roof terrace. The model dates from the New Kingdom, which lasted from about 1550 to 1069 B.C.

This wooden bed was found in the tomb of King Tutankhamen and dates from about 1332 to 1322 B.C.

The insides of wealthy Egyptians' homes were large and were often decorated with bright colors, wall paintings, and plants.

Egyptians used curved wooden (above) or stone headrests as pillows.

Villas

Wealthy Egyptian families lived in large villas outside town. The rooms in the villas had high ceilings and were decorated with colorful wall paintings. These homes included quarters for servants, as well as beautiful gardens and pools stocked with fish. Another privilege that the wealthy enjoyed was to have a bathroom in their home.

The home furnishings of both the rich and the poor were usually simple. Both sat on reed mats and mud benches. They used oil lamps for light. They kept their clothes and earthen pots in wooden chests. The peasants slept on reed mats, however. The wealthy Egyptians had real beds with wooden frames.

Marriage

Ancient Egyptians married young. Girls usually married between ages 12 and 14. Boys would marry once they had a job and could support a family. They were usually about 15. Ancient Egyptians did not trust foreigners. A man would often look for a wife within his town. It was not uncommon for uncles to marry their nieces, and marriages between cousins happened quite often. Statues found in tombs often show couples embracing. This suggests that many couples in ancient Egypt married for love. Arranged marriages were common only in the royal family. Wives and husbands were buried in the same tomb so that they could be together in the afterlife.

Right: *This fresco shows Senefer, the mayor of Thebes and the general for Pharaoh Amenhotep II, seated next to his wife Senay.*

Left: Paintings and sculptures from ancient Egypt often showed the whole family. Here a man sits with his wife and son.

In this carved relief on a tomb doorway, children are shown playing games. This image was created between 2350 and 2190 B.C.

Egyptian parents loved all of their children, but boys were especially important. This is an image of Amenhirkhepshef, the son of Ramses III.

Isis, an Egyptian goddess, cares for her son, Horus. Egyptian kings were thought to be the god Horus in human form.

Children

Even though most families included four or five children, infant deaths were quite common. The children who survived infections or diseases were treasured by their parents. The mother usually nursed her children until they were three. Almost as soon as they could walk, they were expected to help their parents with chores. Boys began to learn their fathers' trade around the age of four. Children also had time to play. They mostly played outdoors with pets or the farm animals. Children also played with balls, sticks, and wooden dolls. Children are shown in tomb art as having shaved heads with a sidelock of hair. They usually did not wear clothes until they were 12.

The Role of Women in the Home

Women received great respect in the home. When she married, the woman became the mistress of the house. Her main role was being a wife. The men made the rules in the house, and the wives had to obey their husbands. However, women had the same legal rights as men. They were able to own property and to get a divorce.

Women usually worked in the home. Each day they fetched water from either the Nile or the nearest canal. They carried the water in huge jugs on their head. They did most of the cooking. Women spent part of their days weaving linen from flax and making clothes. Wealthy people hired servants for housework.

Women carried food by balancing it on their head. The Egyptians enjoyed meals of fruits, vegetables, and grains, as well as the meat from animals or waterfowl that made their homes along the Nile River.

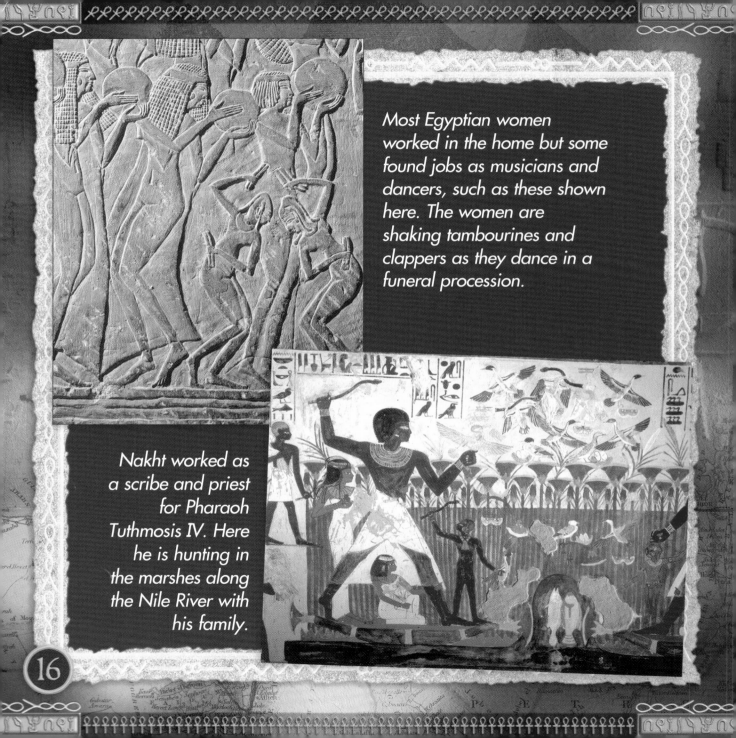

Most Egyptian women worked in the home but some found jobs as musicians and dancers, such as these shown here. The women are shaking tambourines and clappers as they dance in a funeral procession.

Nakht worked as a scribe and priest for Pharaoh Tuthmosis IV. Here he is hunting in the marshes along the Nile River with his family.

From an early age, children in ancient Egypt helped their parents with simple tasks. Children learned from their parents' example. Girls learned how to sew and cook from their mothers. Girls usually did not go to school. Boys usually learned the trade of their fathers, such as carpentry or metalwork. Parents also taught their children in the areas of religion and moral principles. Formal education was a privilege in ancient Egypt. Only boys from rich families attended school. They started when they were four. They would study reading, writing, and math. They usually graduated when they were 14. Many of these boys became scribes.

The land in ancient Egypt was very fertile and produced rich harvests of vegetables and fruit. The ancient Egyptians ate three meals per day. In an ordinary family, the main meal consisted of onions, salted fish, and bread made from ground wheat. Milk was provided by cows and goats. Meat was not as common as fish. Cooked food was often prepared outside or in a separate kitchen. Fish or meat was cooked on a spit over a fire. Before they ate, the ancient Egyptians washed their hands. Both the rich and the poor ate their food using their fingers. The family would sit cross-legged on reed mats around the food, which was placed on a large platter.

Cooks prepare bread in this tomb painting from the Fifth Dynasty, between 2494 and 2345 B.C. Bread was often served as the main meal, even for wealthy Egyptians.

A slave woman helps a guest to put on a lotus necklace. Notice that the slave wears her hair and clothing in a different style than does the guest.

These women are dressed for a banquet, or a large feast. Notice the dark kohl outlines around their eyes.

Egyptians used perfumed oil to moisturize their skin. The perfume was kept in a jar, such as this fancy one found in the tomb of King Tutankhamen.

Personal Hygiene

Ancient Egyptians from all social classes wore similar clothing. Men wore loincloths or short tunics. Women wore simple dresses. Clothes were usually made from linen, which was light and cool on the skin and helped to reduce perspiration in the hot weather.

Ancient Egyptians bathed regularly because of the heat and the dust. They bathed in the river or in a large basin. They used perfumed oil to moisturize their skin. Both men and women used cosmetics. Cosmetics are products applied to the body for decoration. They mixed oil and powder to make kohl. They applied kohl to their eyes to protect them from the dust, the glare of the sun, and diseases.

Religion in the Home

The Egyptians worshiped many gods, and prayed for such things as plentiful harvests and healthy children. Egyptians believed that gods protected them in this world and helped them to reach the next one safely. Most people worshiped the gods at home. They would set up a small shrine or, if they had the space, use one of their rooms as a chapel. A pregnant mother would worship protective gods, such as Bastet, the cat goddess of fertility. The ancient Egyptians tried to please the gods by praying to them every day. However, they could not devote all their time to worship. Life was also filled with concerns about what to eat, whom to marry, and how to raise children.

Glossary

cherish (CHER-ish) To care deeply.

diseases (duh-ZEEZ-ez) Illnesses or sicknesses.

earthen (ER-thun) Made from earth.

fertile (FER-tul) Good for making and growing things.

flax (FLAKS) A fiber that comes from the stem of the flax plant and that can be spun into thread to make linen.

foreigners (FOR-in-urz) People from other countries or places.

fresco (FRES-koh) A painting done on wet plaster. Plaster is a mix of lime, sand, and water that hardens as it dries

hygiene (HY-jeen) The practice of keeping oneself clean.

infections (in-FEK-shunz) Sicknesses caused by germs.

loincloths (LOYN-kloths) Small pieces of material worn around the hips.

perspiration (per-spuh-RAY-shun) Sweat; the action of the body letting out moisture to cool itself.

privilege (PRIV-lij) A special right or favor.

scribes (SKRYBZ) People whose job is to copy books by hand.

shrine (SHRYN) A special place at which prayers or memorials can be made.

spit (SPIT) A metal rod that holds meat over a fire for cooking.

survived (sur-VYVD) Stayed alive.

tombs (TOOMZ) Graves.

tunics (TOO-niks) Large, loose shirts.

Index

B
bathroom, 9
benches, 9

C
children, 5, 13, 17, 22
chores, 5, 13
cosmetics, 21

D
diseases, 13
divorce, 14

E
education, 17

F
flax, 14

G
gods, 5, 22

L
lamps, 9
linen, 21

M
marriages, 10
milk, 18
mud bricks, 6

N
Nile River, 6, 14

P
pets, 5
play, 13

T
tomb(s), 5, 10
town houses, 6

V
villas, 9

Primary Sources

Cover. Bearers bring geese to an offering table. Detail from painting from tomb of Nakht, a scribe and priest under Pharaoh Tuthmosis IV. 18th Dynasty. Circa 1421–1413 B.C. **Inset.** Bastet, patron goddess of Bubastis, as a cat. Bronze figure with inlaid blue glass eyes. 713–332 B.C. **Page 4.** Akhenaton, Nefertiti and their three daughters worshiping the sun god Aton. Household shrine found near Amarna. Painted limestone stele. Circa 1350 B.C. **Page 7. Left.** Model house with two stories and roof terrace. Terra-cotta. Circa 1539–1075 B.C. **Right.** Household furniture. Wood, rush, and palm. Circa 1550–1295 B.C. **Page 8. Top.** Wooden bed from the tomb of Tutankhamen. Circa 1332–1322 B.C. **Right.** Wooden headrest. 5th Dynasty. **Page 11. Top.** Senefer and his wife Senay. Fresco from the tomb of Senefer, mayor of Thebes and general pharaoh Amenhotep II. 1450–1425 B.C. **Bottom left.** Neferhebef with his wife and son. Painted limestone. Circa 1539–1075 B.C. **Page 12. Top.** Children playing games. Reliefs from a doorway in the tomb of Mereuka. Circa 2350–2190 B.C. **Bottom left.** Fresco in the tomb of Amenhirkhepshef, 20th Dynasty Egyptian prince, son of Ramses III. Circa 1194–63 B.C. **Page 15.** Women carrying food on their heads. Bas–relief from tomb of Ti, 5th Dynasty official serving in the reign of Kakai. Circa 2446–2426 B.C. **Page 16. Top.** Women playing tambourines, girls shaking clappers, dancing, from funerary procession. Limestone relief. Circa 1300–1200 B.C. **Bottom.** Nakht with his family hunting in the Nile marshes. Detail of wallpainting in the tomb of Nakht. 16th to 14th centuries B.C. **Page 19.** Cooks preparing and cooking bread. From tomb of Nefer and Ka–Hay. Circa 2494–2345 B.C. **Page 20. Top.** Slave girl of Rekhmire's household helps a guest put on a lotus necklace. Detail of a wallpainting in the tomb of Rekhmire. Circa 1479–1400 B.C. **Bottom left.** Ladies offering a lemon and a mandragora root to another lady during a banquet. Detail of a wallpainting in the tomb of Nakht. 18th Dynasty. **Bottom right.** Perfume jar with papyrus motif. Alabaster. From the tomb of Tutankhamen. 18th Dynasty.

Web Sites

Due to the changing nature of Internet links, PowerKids Press has developed an online list of Web sites related to the subject of this book. This site is updated regularly. Please use this link to access the list:
www.powerkidslinks.com/psaciv/homeegy/